POWELL

Evans

EVANS BROTHERS LIMITED

Evans Brothers LImited
2A Portman Mansions
Chiltern Street
London W1M 1LE

©Evans Brothers Limited 1999

First published 1999

British Library Cataloguing in Publication Data.

Powell, Jillian
    Family matters. - (Life Files)
    1.Family - Juvenile literature
    2.Marriage - Juvenile literature
    I.Title
    306.8

ISBN 0 237 51886 4 (hardback)

ACKNOWLEDGEMENTS

Editorial: Christopher Westhorp
Design: Tinstar Design (www.tinstar.co.uk)
Production: Jenny Mulvanny

For permission to reproduce copyright material the
Author and Publishers gratefully acknowledge the
following:
Cover Tony Stone Images/Elie Bernager **page 7**
Collections/Anthea Sieveking **page 8** Tony Stone
Images/Paul Chesley **page 9** Panos Pictures/Irene
Sleat **page 11** Robert Harding Picture Library/Robin
Hanbury-Tenison **page 13** Panos Pictures/Philip
Wolmuth **page 15** Tony Stone Images/Ranald
Mackechnie **page 16** Collections/Anthea Sieveking
page 19 Hutchison Library/Melanie Friend **page 20**
Tony Stone/Tony Latham **page 22** Hutchison Library/
Robert Francis **page 23** Tony Stone Images/Stewart
Cohen **page 24** Tony Stone Images/Nicholas DeVore
page 25 Tony Stone Images/Frank Herholdt **page 26**
Collections/Liz Stares **page 28** Collections/ Ute
Klaphake **page 29** Tony Stone Images/Jerome Tisne
page 30 Tony Stone Images/Ken Fisher **page 31**
Hutchison Library/N. Durrell McKenna **page 33**
Collections/Anthea Sieveking **page 35** Collections/
Anthea Sieveking **page 37** Panos/Mark McEvoy **page
39** Panos/Neil Cooper **page 42** Tony Stone Images/
Zigy Kaluzny **page 43** Tony Stone Images/David Leach
page 45 Tony Stone Images/Penny Tweedie **page 47**
Tony Stone Images/Penny Gentieu **page 49** Tony Stone
Images/Steven Peters **page 50** Tony Stone Images/
Kevin Horan **page 53** Collections/Anthea Sieveking
page 55 Panos Pictures/Penny Tweedie **page 56** Tony
Stone Images/Tamara Reynolds

CONTENTS

INTRODUCTION

Families are important to all of us. Whether we are part of, or apart from them, love them or hate them, our families help shape our lives and our outlook. But the family is changing. We can no longer expect the continuity of family life that our grandparents and parents enjoyed. Statistics show that while weddings remain popular, the institution of marriage is under threat, and as numbers of divorces and remarriages go on rising, so more people become part of extended stepfamilies. Some predictions suggest that by the year 2010, living in a stepfamily will have become the norm.

These developments have made the family a political as well as a social issue. Problems such as rising levels of crime, delinquency, poor educational achievement and drugs have all been linked to a breakdown in traditional family values. Fierce debates have been sparked by issues such as welfare benefits for lone parents, and parental responsibility for children's misbehaviour and crimes. These issues affect us all as we grow up and take on adult responsibilities ourselves. Family Matters asks you to consider some of the major concerns surrounding the family: Is the family breaking down? Does it matter if it is? Are there any alternatives to the family? It puts forward both sides of the argument on controversial topics such as same-sex parenting and providing IVF treatment to post-menopausal women. These are issues which seem set to change our concepts of the family, and society, into the new millennium. This book invites you to make up your mind about issues which affect every one of us.

WHAT DO WE MEAN BY 'FAMILY MATTERS'?

The family is going through unprecedented change. Four out of ten new marriages currently end in divorce; marriage rates and birth rates are declining, while the numbers of divorces and lone-parent families continue to rise. Many people, including politicians and religious leaders, have expressed concern over the breakdown of traditional family values. Yet in spite of these trends, most of us still grow up in families. When we become adults, most of us will start new families of our own. The Family Policy Studies Centre estimates that in the year 2000, three quarters of the UK population will be married and three quarters of children will live with both their parents until adulthood.

The family gives us a sense of identity and belonging. Members of families are people we should be able to love and trust. Family life helps make us the people we are, and loss or breakdown of our family can have life-long psychological effects. Family life is private, but it becomes a matter of public concern through issues like domestic violence, poor parenting and child abuse. Recently, family change has been blamed for rising levels of youth crime, poor educational achievement and related social problems. There have been calls for more government intervention to support the family, including better provision of childcare, and education in parenting skills.

Families give a sense of identity and belonging to each generation. Many of our basic values and attitudes are shaped by our family background.

WHAT IS A FAMILY?

Families are made up of people who are related to each other by blood, marriage or adoption. The ties which hold families together include:

- blood and kinship
- the law: legal marriage, adoption and registration of birth
- religious vows
- a social sense of obligation, sometimes called family duty, loyalty or honour.

Many societies use ceremony and ritual to mark important events in family life. In tribal societies, these may include coming-of-age, marriage and death ceremonies, which are marked with special foods, dancing, singing and other rituals. In Western societies, where the extended family is in decline, family events such as weddings, funerals and christenings may be the only occasions on which extended families gather together.

In the past, bonds between family members were reinforced by the rituals and traditions which surrounded these important events. In the nineteenth century, it was usual to wear black for a whole year in mourning a close family relative. When someone died, the body was often kept at home and the family maintained a vigil, or watch, until the day of the funeral. Today, care of the dying and dead is often in the hands of professionals such as hospital and hospice staff, doctors and undertakers. For the family in Western cultures, death has become more of a taboo than it was a century ago.

Family ties remain strongest in communities which retain traditional religious and cultural values, such as Catholic, Jewish and Muslim communities. They remain strong among many ethnic minorities living overseas in Western societies, as well as in communities based on blood and kinship, like the Mafia in Italy.

The word 'family' can also be used to describe closeness between people, communities or countries, as when we talk about 'a family of nations'. The terms 'sister'

Jewish communities retain strong family ties. This boy is celebrating his bar mitzvah with members of his family near the Western (Wailing) Wall in Jerusalem's Old City.

and 'brother' are used as expressions of comradeship and solidarity in the Feminist and Socialist movements, and in religious and trade union organisations.

> Traditional society is composed of only two kinds of people – relatives and strangers. The social world centres around kinship identities, and relatives are those with whom you work, worship, ally, sleep, play and die. Kinsmen bear you, nurse you in illness, initiate you into adulthood, protect you from injustice, and bring you into the order of the ancestors.
>
> D.W. Murry *Poor Suffering Bastards: An Anthropologist Looks at Illegitimacy* 1994

WHY DO WE NEED FAMILIES?

The family is a social institution that affects all our lives. Its main purposes are:

- to care for babies and children while they are growing up
- to regulate sexual behaviour
- to socialise children, teaching them the roles they will play in later life as well as basic rules of behaviour, ideas and values
- to care for old, sick and disabled members. In developing countries which do not have an adequate welfare system, those who work support those in their family who cannot.

HOW DO CONCEPTS OF FAMILY DIFFER AROUND THE WORLD?

Families or kinship groups are recognised in almost all societies. Concepts of family differ around the world. They are governed by rules or laws which say who can and cannot marry, and who has the right to inherit property and titles. Arranged marriages still take place in some parts of the world within certain cultures and religions. In some developing countries, young children may be pledged in marriage to secure land, property or social status. Ideas which may be taboo in some cultures, are permitted in others. Whereas many cultures forbid incest, or sexual relations between family members, the Balinese of Indonesia allow twins to marry, as they believe they have been intimate in the womb.

Kinship groups are the oldest type of family organisation. In Africa and Asia, they include all the blood relations of the head of the group and may occupy a whole village. Some are based on father-son relationships, as among the Tiv people of Nigeria; others, like the Yao tribe in Malawi, are based on mother-daughter relationships.

In a number of African countries, like Kenya, and in some Muslim societies, polygamy – where a man can marry more than one wife – is still permitted, although this practice is declining. Polyandry – where a wife may have several husbands – is rarer, although it is still found among nomadic peoples of Nepal and Tibet. In the Toda culture of southern India, a woman who marries also becomes the wife of her husband's brothers. A Toda husband can establish his paternity of a child by presenting the wife with ritual gifts. In societies where there is communal ownership of property, less importance is attached to biological parentage. A child may have a 'social parent', such as a maternal uncle, who is responsible for the child's upbringing and acts as a father role model.

> **❝** Very few issues in contemporary society have been the subject of such scrutiny as 'the family'. Such intense interest as we have seen over recent months reflects not only people's obvious interest in a topic of everyday relevance to themselves, but also that unease that something, somewhere, is not right. **❞**
>
> Alistair Burt, *Families and the Future*, 1995

Religious and legal ceremonies create family ties. In this Buddhist wedding ceremony in Thailand, two women are marrying one man to create a family unit.

The Yanomami Indians of the Amazon basin form a tribal society in which several families may live together in communal dwellings.

> ❝ Not only has there never been an open, democratic society not based on the family, there has never been any society of any sort not based on the family. ❞
>
> M. Levy *Feminism and Freedom* 1987

Find out!

Design a questionnaire to establish definitions of the family. It could take the form of questions or a list of statements to be ranked in order, e.g. 'The family is a married couple living with children.'

WHAT ARE THE ALTERNATIVES TO THE FAMILY?

The Kibbutz movement in Israel replaces the nuclear family unit with group or community living. (Kibbutz means 'group' in Hebrew.) Kibbutzim are communities based around farming co-operatives. They were set up on socialist principles after the state of Israel was founded in 1948. They aimed to create equality between men and women by organising communal childcare, freeing women to work alongside men. Children on a commune are brought up in separate accommodation, and although they see their parents for part of the day, other adults share their childcare. Each member works for the group as a whole, sharing community tasks and eating meals together. Only a tiny proportion of the Israeli population now live in Kibbutzim and it has become more common for children to live with their parents in self-contained units within the community.

The Commune movement was part of the hippie 'counter-culture' of the 1960s and 1970s in Europe and the US. Communes were experiments in group living set up by young people who rejected mainstream culture and a value system based on consumerism and competition. Communes were often housed on derelict farms or in old country houses with land for growing crops. Some aimed to be self-sufficient. Members shared chores, meals and games. Some believed in sharing property and sexual partners, and practised group marriages and communal child rearing.

New Age travellers emerged in the 1980s and 1990s. Groups live in vans or caravans, moving from place to place to follow music festivals or eco-campaigns such as fighting the building of new motorways or the export of live animals. Their lifestyle takes inspiration from centuries-old gypsy traditions as well as the Commune movement.

Fewer people today are experimenting with group or community living, but more are choosing to live alone. According to the Office for National Statistics' *Social Trends for 1996/7*, more than a quarter of UK households are now occupied by people living alone. This is double the proportion recorded in 1961. By 2020, it is forecast that most women in the UK will be living alone. Currently, the fastest growing group of single householders is men under the age of sixty-five. As people live longer, and there are more divorces, and more people choosing to remain single and childless, the number of people who choose to live alone is predicted to go on rising.

> 66 Most people are brought up to think that there is no alternative to living in families if one wishes to seek personal fulfilment and happiness in life. 99

Question
What do you think are the pros and cons of living in a commune?

Question
What do you think are the pros and cons of living alone?

VIEWS ON THE FAMILY

The family has been much in the news lately. Divorces of high-profile figures, including royals and media stars, have made family breakdown headline news. Politicians and religious leaders have blamed the loss of traditional family values for rising crime rates and related social problems including delinquency, drugs and vandalism. In the early 1990s, reports of domestic violence, children left 'home alone' and the shocking case of the murder of a toddler by two ten-year-old boys focused attention on the 'dysfunctional family'. It became the subject of serious documentaries, comedy, and even cartoons like *The Simpsons*.

In debates about the family, some people argue that family values are the key to a civilised society. Others see a dark side to the family. They believe it can be a damaging and stifling environment, harbouring domestic violence and physical and emotional abuse. Sociologists have developed these ideas into different theories or views on the family.

Some people argue that many of society's problems are caused by the loss of traditional values. Some poor families, and lone mothers, live in temporary hostel accommodation, adding to the pressures on them and, in some cases, contributing to dysfunctional behaviour.

> **Nearly 100,000 teenage pregnancies every year. Elderly parents with whom families cannot cope. Children growing up without role models they can respect and learn from. More and deeper poverty. More crime. More truancy. More neglect of educational opportunities. And above all, more unhappiness.**
>
> Tony Blair, UK Prime Minister, 30 September 1997

and smallholdings, so the modern family has evolved to serve industry. Today, the family is socially isolated and geographically mobile. It is still evolving, as more women work and men take a more active role in the home and childcare, creating the 'symmetrical family'.

> **Whatever route you take to explain the violence on the streets, unemployment, 1960s' free love, feminism, capitalism or its absence, most analysts now come back to the idea of the traditional family.**
>
> Jonathan Margolis *The Sunday Times* 7 March 1993

FUNCTIONALISM

Functionalists believe that the nuclear family fits the needs of an industrial society. They see society as an organism made up from social institutions like the family, religion and the economic system. The family is a vital part, like the heart and brains of a body, and its two main purposes are:

- to socialise children, teaching them the roles they will play in adult life
- to stabilise adult relationships and personalities.

Functionalists believe that in its ideal form, the family consists of a nuclear unit of husband, wife and children. Their roles are different but complementary. Just as the extended family was functional in pre-industrial times, when the whole family worked together on labour-intensive farms

MARXISTS

Marxists see the family as serving the interests of the capitalist ruling classes. Families make men into wage slaves, rear children as a future labour force, and keep women in a subservient role doing unpaid labour in the home. This view was first put forward by Friedrich Engels in *The Origin of Family, Private Property and the State*, published in 1884. Engels believed that property ownership, of land for crops and later for houses and factories, produced patriarchal societies with men dominating subservient women and children. Marxists see the family as reflecting inequalities in the rest of society. They believe that the exploitation and oppression of the family can only be ended by political revolution, replacing capitalism with a communist or socialist society. Some of Engels' ideas about sharing property and greater sexual equality and freedom were taken up by members of the Commune movement in Europe and the US in the 1960s and 1970s.

> **❝** If the respect afforded to the privacy of a family is at the expense of the respect afforded to an individual's rights within it, then the question arises whether or not that is too high a cost to be paid. **❞**
>
> Lorna J.F. Smith, *Domestic Violence* Home Office Research Study, 1989

> **❝** The irony is that privacy contributes to, and reinforces, the intimacy and sense of solidarity of family life that society values, while it also nurtures and protects the very conditions in which conflict and violence develop. **❞**
>
> M. Borkowski *Marital Violence* 1985

MARXIST-FEMINISTS

Marxist-feminists focus on the oppression of women by the family in capitalist economies. They believe that capitalism exploits the unpaid labour of women as wives and mothers to keep wage costs down. A woman's role in the family is to serve her husband and bear children to be the next generation of wage slaves. Marxist-feminists believe that in a socialist society, men and women would work alongside one another equally, sharing responsibilities for home and childcare.

Feminists argue that the responsibilities of caring for home and children should be shared equally between men and women.

Question
'True liberation for women can only come about with the abolition of the family.' Do you think this is true?

FEMINISTS

Feminists see the family not as a voluntary unit based on love and choice but as an economic unit which makes women dependent on men. It is not efficient because many women, children and old people depend on support from the state. Feminists see the key to change in the relationships between men and women. Liberal feminists think that this can be achieved gradually, by persuading men to take a more active part in housework and child rearing. They believe there should be laws to create equal opportunities and that children should be educated into a culture of equality. Radical feminists think that women will only be liberated by abolishing the family and patriarchal societies. They campaign for wages for housework and for tough legislation on issues like domestic violence. Some radical feminists are lesbians. They argue for women's liberation from men through lesbian relationships, using sperm donors and artificial insemination for reproduction.

Question
Do you think women should be paid wages for housework and childcare?

In spite of changing roles, many women are still responsible for domestic work in the home.

The New Right

The New Right includes conservative political and religious groups and thinkers. They see the conventional nuclear family as the key to a healthy society, and believe that many social problems today are caused by a decline in traditional family values. New Right concerns include:

- increasing sexual permissiveness
- rising rates of divorce and marital breakdown
- a rise in the number of co-habiting couples
- a rise in the number of births outside marriage
- a rise in the number of lone-parent families.

They link these trends to:

- rising crime rates
- juvenile delinquency and vandalism
- drug abuse
- poor educational achievement
- dependency on welfare benefits

The New Right believes that the tax and welfare systems should be used to discourage lone parenthood and that there should be legislation to pursue absent fathers for child maintenance. They believe that married parents, with mothers responsible for the home and childcare, provide the most stable environment for children to grow up in. These ideas were put forward by the Conservative government in the UK in their 'Back to Basics' campaign of the early 1990s, which looked to a 'Golden Age' of the Victorian past for traditional family values.

> " The decline of the traditional family unit is happening at a point in history when, despite the fact that we are materially richer than 50 years ago, we are considerably more anxious, ten times more likely to suffer from depression, with 20 per cent of the population developing a serious mental illness at some point in their lifetime. "
>
> Libby Brooks *The Guardian* 15 October 1997

Find out!

Carry out a questionnaire among friends and relations to explore how the ideas of the New Right are viewed. Do you think that the New Right approach to the family reflects popular opinion?

> " The family is the natural and fundamental group unit of society and is entitled to protection by society and the State. "
>
> Article 16 (3) of the Universal Declaration of Human Rights, United Nations, 1948

PSYCHIATRIC CRITICS

Psychiatrists explore 'the dark side of the family'. They criticise the close-knit nuclear family for being too inward-looking, caring only for its members, and believe that it can be negative and destructive. They focus on issues like domestic violence and abuse, and believe that the main victims of the family are women and children. Psychiatrists also point out that the majority of child abuse cases take place within the family. They believe that in the nuclear family, parents exercise a stifling control over their children, preventing their development as free-thinking individuals. In the 1960s, the psychiatrists R.D. Laing and David Cooper suggested that repressive family life could also be responsible for mental illnesses, including schizophrenia. The work of psychiatric critics and sociologists on the negative aspects of family life has led to the development of family therapy and counselling, which aims to help individuals and families explore and resolve the tensions and problems of family life.

Question

'For children to stand the best chance of thriving in our culture they need, ideally, to experience the unconditional love of a mother and a father who are committed both to the child and to each other.' (Richard Whitfield, Chairman of the National Family Trust, writing in *Community Care* magazine.) What do you think?

HOW HAS FAMILY STRUCTURE CHANGED?

Throughout the twentieth century, the birth rate in developed countries has been falling. Three generations ago, families of four, six or even ten children were common. During the 1970s, the birth rate in the UK fell by a quarter, reaching an average 2.4 children per family by 1995. In the UK today, one- or two-child families have become the norm. The century has also seen increasing geographical and social mobility (encouraged by wide ownership of cars), job insecurity and the growing influence of technology on our lives.

In the past, nuclear family units often lived a few doors away from members of the extended family, such as grandparents, uncles and aunts. Jobs like coalmining and shipbuilding were passed down through the generations and many people remained near their birthplace for the whole of their lives. Today, young people are more likely to move away in search of work, even abroad, although they may stay in touch with their extended family through regular visits and telephone calls.

In China, one-child family units, such as this one in Beijing, reflect government policy rather than parental choice.

Question

The Chinese government restricts families to one child only and there are fines for anyone disobeying the rules. With global population expanding, do you think this is responsible family policy or a serious infringement of human rights?

> ❝ The family is alive and kicking. It is extremely elastic, and is able to stretch to encompass all sorts of people within it. ❞
>
> Francis McGlone, Senior Researcher, Family Policy Studies Centre

Question

'We must emphasise our belief that the traditional two-parent family is best. Best for the parents, best for society and above all best for children.'
(Michael Howard, then UK Home Secretary, 5 October 1993.)
Do you agree?

Is the Traditional Nuclear Family in Decline?

Some sociologists have detected a trend through this century towards smaller, more isolated, private family units, although these may no longer consist of the traditional pattern of breadwinner husband, dependent wife and children. Statistics show that in the US today, under four per cent of families conform to this pattern. In the UK, in the past thirty years, the proportion of traditional family units of parents and dependent children in the population as a whole has fallen from more than a third to a quarter. The rising rates of divorce and separation, growth in the number of lone-parent families, and the increase in people choosing to co-habit rather than marry, or to live alone, have all contributed to a decline of the traditional nuclear family unit, and a corresponding increase in the diversity of small household units.

Changing social attitudes have offered women new choices, in whether to have a career and in what sort of career to pursue. It is no longer expected that all women will want to marry and raise children.

> **" In Britain today, it is clear that the family is facing increasing pressures and difficulties, with changing family structures and different expectations at work, at home and in society. "**
>
> The late Diana, Princess of Wales, United Nations Year of the Family, 1994

Asian households in the UK are extended family units – these families may keep traditional values and practices such as arranged marriages, but there is evidence that these are declining under the influence of Western ideas and values.

Find out!
In Bengal, where the extended family is still important, there are fifty-three terms for a relative. How many can you think of in English?

Question
'The family – the conventional couple with two kids idealised by advertisers and moral conservatives – is on its last lap.'
Do you think this is true?

WHAT ARE THE TRENDS WORLDWIDE?

Worldwide, the trend is towards smaller family units. There has been a decline in clans and corporate kin groups, the oldest kind of family organisation. In China, the old Tsu system of kinship and landholding was abolished after the establishment of communist rule in 1949, giving way to single-child nuclear units. Extended family units remain more important in developing countries and in ethnic communities which still hold strong cultural and religious values. In the developing world, the larger size of family units reflects high infant mortality rates, labour-intensive farming methods and the need for child labour to support the family. Among ethnic communities living overseas, extended family units reflect strong family ties and values, and help to support members with low wages and insecure employment prospects. Just over one fifth of

> **" Huge changes in the fabric of the family have taken place throughout most of the developed world since the mid-developed world since the decline of 60s, bringing about the decline of the nuclear family and the undermining of marriage. This period of social upheaval, without parallel since the Industrial Revolution, I call the 'Great Disruption'. "**
>
> Francis Fukuyama *The End of Order* 1997

WHAT INFLUENCES FAMILY STRUCTURE?

Family structure evolves under the influence of a range of factors. These include:

•Legislation and social policy

Some countries, like Germany and Sweden, have social policies relating directly to the family. In the UK there was debate during the 1980s as to how far the government should interfere with family life, becoming a 'Nanny State'. Social policy on issues such as divorce, lone parents, sexual equality, paternal rights, employment laws and care of the elderly all influence and shape the family. In the UK, major changes in the divorce laws in 1969 have sharply increased divorce rates over the last thirty years. Cuts in public funding for pensions and care homes have shifted the responsibility for care of the elderly and the sick on to the community and the family. Legislation on sexual equality and employment have increased women's roles in the workplace, although a lower proportion of women work full-time in the UK than in France, where childcare is more easily available.

This Japanese couple have chosen Waikiki in Oahu, Hawaii, for their wedding, reflecting the fashionable trend in the developed world towards exotic locations for marriage ceremonies.

• Loss of religious belief and values

The secularisation of society has also changed family structure. Even in Roman Catholic countries, the influence of religion on issues like divorce and abortion is declining. In the West, more people are choosing to co-habit rather than make marriage vows before God. More of those who do marry do so in venues other than a church. According to the Office for National Statistics' figures, the number of people in England and Wales marrying in venues other than a church or a register office has recently increased fourfold.

• Advances in medical technology

The introduction of the birth-control pill in the 1960s, and legislation in some countries permitting abortion, meant that for the first time women were able to control their own reproductive cycles. This increased sexual activity outside marriage, reduced the number of unwanted pregnancies and contributed to a decline in the birth rate. Advances in reproductive technologies such as *in vitro* (see page 57) fertilisation and artificial insemination have meant that more infertile couples and older women are able to have children.

• Changes in social attitudes

Dramatic changes in social attitudes in the last thirty years have created opportunities for a diverse range of family patterns and a greater choice in the way people live their lives. In Western society, divorce and lone parenthood have become acceptable. Awareness of gay rights has increased the number of gay couples applying to foster and adopt children, or choosing to parent their own children through artificial insemination or surrogacy. The influence of feminist thought from the 1960s and 1970s has altered women's expectations and challenged traditional roles of male breadwinner and dependent housewife and mother.

• Demographic changes

People are living longer and spending a shorter proportion of their lives rearing children. Women are having fewer children, and having them later or remaining childless. One in ten women born in the 1940s remained childless but this figure is expected to double in the next generation. The number of women remaining unmarried is also increasing. In 1971, four per cent of women remained unmarried by the age of fifty; this had more than quadrupled by 1987. Overall, the Office for National Statistics' *Social Trends* showed that in 1996–97, more than a quarter of UK households were occupied by one person – double the proportion recorded in 1961.

More women are now choosing to remain single and childless, evidenced by an overall rise in the number of single-occupier households.

INCREASED PROSPERITY

In developed countries, increased wealth has encouraged smaller family units. From the Middle Ages onwards, children were regarded as future earners, and big families were seen as productive units. Children and adults worked together, helping with the care of crops and animals. The labour-intensive system of farming required as many helpers as possible, especially at times like harvest. The Industrial Revolution, and in the late twentieth century the Technological Revolution, both drastically reduced the need for labour. In developed countries, compulsory schooling and restrictions on child labour have reduced the need for large families, although in developing countries the extended family is still seen as a productive unit, bringing greater wealth. Recently, there have been calls for investigations into the exploitation of child labour to produce cheap goods for Western markets.

> " Change need not always be bad, but recent changes have made the family a less stable environment, a less secure place to raise a child. Stability is important in a child's life and stability is provided by the strength of the parents' relationship. "
>
> Alistair Burt *Families and the Future* 1995

Question

Do you think we should boycott goods produced by child labour in developing countries?

These young Moroccan children are working at dye vats to colour sheepskins. Lack of legislation means that child labour is still exploited in many developing countries.

HOW HAVE FAMILY LIFESTYLES CHANGED?

The twentieth century has brought many changes to the way families live, work and spend their leisure time. In the prosperous developed world, homes are generally less crowded and more comfortable than they were 100 years ago. People are better fed, healthier and have a longer life expectancy. Family life underwent significant changes during the Industrial Revolution of the eighteenth and nineteenth centuries. In 1801, when the first UK census was carried out, only 20 per cent of the population lived in towns or cities, but 100 years later four times as many were living in urban areas. In the twentieth century, the Technological Revolution has brought increasingly rapid change to family lifestyles.

> **As the pace of technology accelerates, so the pressures and demands placed on our children rise. We expect our children to somehow cope with a world of technology that our grandparents hardly dreamt of.**
>
> Jon Bernardes *Children in Families* Family Studies, 1997

Traditional family activities, such as playing board games together, are increasingly threatened by solitary pursuits like computer games.

HOW HAS TECHNOLOGY CHANGED OUR LIVES?

Mass ownership of cars, and faster transport by air, rail and sea, have made families and individuals more mobile, taking us further afield both for work and leisure. Cars have made holidays and day trips to shopping malls, theme parks and safari parks a regular part of family life. Forty years ago, only a minority of families owned a car. In the past twenty years this has changed and now not only do three quarters of households have a car, but a quarter have two or more.

Three generations ago, many family holidays were restricted to a day at the seaside. Today, jet travel and package deals have made holidays abroad, even to long-haul destinations, available to many. *The Family Expenditure Survey* of 1996–97 found that families in the UK allowed five per cent of their leisure spending for holidays. They took fifty-four million holidays in 1996, with an increasing number having two or more holidays a year.

The car, along with a wide range of household appliances and gadgets, including mobile phones, televisions with remote controls and home computers, has made us much less active than we used to be. Shopping used to involve walking to different shops, including greengrocers, bakers and butchers. Many people now do all their shopping under one roof at a supermarket, often at an out-of-town shopping centre or mall, where restaurants and children's play areas have made shopping into a major leisure activity.

Find out!
Ask two generations of your family how they used to spend their leisure time when they were your age. How is it different? Were they more or less active than you are?

Question
'By its domination of the time families spend together it (television) destroys the special qualities that distinguish one family from another.' (M. Winn. *The Plug-in Drug*, 1985.) Do you agree?

Modern town planning, out-of-town shopping centres and the supermarket have all made the car an essential part of family life.

Question

Do you think your experience of childhood was very different from your parents' or grandparents'? If so, how?

HOW HAS HOME LIFE CHANGED?

HOW HAS FAMILY SPENDING CHANGED?

Annual figures for the *General Household Survey* show that as families become more prosperous, the proportion of income spent on leisure and entertainment increases.

Between 1971 and 1996, family spending on recreation and entertainment trebled. There has been a rapid increase in the ownership of household appliances and electronic goods. These include labour-saving appliances like washing machines and dishwashers, which make household tasks faster and easier, and home-based entertainment facilities like video recorders, CD players and home computers.

In 1995 the most sought after possessions were CD players, owned by half of households, and microwaves, owned by nearly three quarters. In the decade from 1986 to 1996, the number of households owning a video recorder more than doubled to 82 per cent. Mobile phones and home computers are now increasingly sought after, with one in five households owning a mobile phone in 1997, and one in twenty households owning a computer with an internet link.

In the past, the fireside or 'hearth' was the focal point of family life. To the Romans it was the dwelling place of the household gods, and in British folklore it was the home of the fairies or brownies who brought good luck to the household. When a family moved home, it was traditional to take embers from the old fireplace to the new, to symbolise family ties remaining unbroken. In the 1930s and 1940s, many families spent their leisure time sitting by the fire, listening to the radio. Central heating, which began to be used in the UK during the 1960s, did away with many fireplaces, and television has replaced the fireplace as the focus of many family rooms.

Central heating and mass ownership of two or more television sets, mean that families are less likely to gather together in leisure time. Children spend more time in their rooms, playing with computers or watching their own televisions. A MORI survey in the UK in 1996 found that eight out of ten teenagers had a television in their bedrooms. In the US, around twenty hours a week, or half of the average leisure time, is spent watching television. Joint family activities – such as singing round the piano, which was common in the nineteenth century, or playing cards and board games, popular entertainments during the inter-war years – have been replaced by things we do on our own, such as using home computers and playstations or listening to music on individual headsets.

HOW HAVE CHILDREN'S LIVES CHANGED?

In many ways, children enjoy more freedom and rights than they did in past generations, when they were required to be 'seen but not heard'. The media have created a 'youth culture', giving young people their own clothes, magazines, music and television programmes. Sports and leisure clubs offer a wide range of activities from super bowl to roller blading and kart racing. At home, as described, many children have their own televisions, music systems and computers. These have made them less active than children used to be, when they walked or cycled to school and spent their free time playing outdoors. Today, children in the UK watch an average of twenty-eight hours television a week, and computer games are a favourite leisure activity. Cars, urban living and parents' increased concern for children's safety have made children less free to roam. In inner cities, playing on the streets can expose children to drug-dealing, vandalism and crime.

Question

'We should no longer class children as rich or poor, advantaged or disadvantaged, but as caged or free-range.' Do you think that you enjoy more or less freedom than your parents did when they were children?

A modern child's bedroom can be a self-contained entertainment complex, with a television, computer, video recorder, music centre and games machines.

WHY IS THE FAMILY MEAL DECLINING?

In the past, sitting down together around a table to eat was an important part of family life. Family meals are also central to many religious and secular festivals such as Christmas, the Jewish Passover and, in the US, Thanksgiving. In the UK, Mothering Sunday used to be a time for children to return to the family home for a special meal. A 1993 Mintel survey found that only half of families in the UK sit down to a family meal in the evening. More than a third of all families eat in front of the television. There is also a tendency for families to 'snack and graze', with members of the family eating different meals at different times. There is a growing market for ready meals, snacks, individual portions, slimmer's meals and children's meals. According to a Henley Centre survey, the average time spent cooking has been reduced by over an hour a week since 1985. As more wives and mothers work – and women remain the chief providers of meals – there has been a growth in convenience foods like cook-chill and microwave meals. Fast foods and takeaways have become part of family lifestyle. Trips to 'burger bars' are a popular family treat.

> ❝ We should value the family meal more because it's the only time when parents and children get together. Everyone might be tired and stressed, but sharing those experiences is what family life is about. ❞
>
> Dr Richard Woolfson, child psychologist and author, *The Observer* 5 February 1998

Question

Do you think it matters that the family meal is declining? If so, why?

Sharing a meal can be an important part of family life.

HOW DO ADVERTISEMENTS MIRROR FAMILY LIFESTYLE?

Since the 1950s, the advertising industry has targeted the family as consumers for a wide range of products including food, clothes, babycare, household cleaners, electronic goods and gadgets. Children have become especially 'brand-aware', targeted for brand-name products like jeans and training shoes, as well as food products including burgers, sweets and crisps. In the 1950s, the industry created the 'cereal packet family' of mother, father, boy and girl, and although this image still persists there are now attempts to represent 'politically correct' role models, such as working women, men doing household chores or caring for children, and older people enjoying an active retirement.

> 66 **The mundane tasks of cooking, eating and clearing up – such central activities within any domestic regime – are curiously absent from existing sociological descriptions of family life.** 99
>
> J. Burgoyne and D. Clark *The Sociology of Food and Eating* 1985

Find out!

How far do you think advertisers accurately reflect today's family lifestyle? Choose examples from television and magazines to argue your case.

Advertising images create an ideal of family life which is sometimes called 'the cereal packet family'.

HOW HAVE FAMILY RELATIONSHIPS CHANGED?

As changes in family structure and patterns have taken place, so have changes in relationships within the family. Relationships between partners, between parents and children, and between the old and the young have all changed due to a range of factors including changes in the law, in the tax and welfare systems, in education, ideas and attitudes.

Women's roles have undergone the most dramatic changes. Women are living longer, having fewer children (or remaining childless) and giving birth later. With life expectancy continuing to increase, child rearing is now taking up a smaller proportion of their lives. The influence of feminist thought, which emerged in the 1960s and 1970s, and the increasing importance of technology in our lives have been two important factors for change.

In the extended family, each generation has its role to play. The Mediterranean countries, such as Spain and Italy, remain more traditional in their family structure.

The changing role of women within the family, with the majority of wives and mothers going out to work and achieving more control over their lives, has in turn changed attitudes to men's roles within the family. Some sociologists have identified the 'symmetrical family', where domestic labour is divided more equally between partners. But many research surveys suggest that 'New Man' was a media creation rather than a reality.

Is New Man a Myth?

Since the idea of 'New Man' was first introduced in the 1970s, there has been an increased awareness of the need for a shift towards greater equality in the division of domestic chores and childcare. 'Politically correct' advertisements show men doing household tasks such as washing clothes, cleaning bathrooms and feeding the baby. With more women now taking on the role of breadwinner in the family, the term 'house husband' has been coined for men who, through choice or unemployment, stay at home and adopt the role of housekeeper and childcarer. Paternity leave has become a political issue, with the UK government planning to introduce a week's paid paternity leave, and the right to three months' unpaid leave. But recent surveys suggest that women retain the bulk of domestic and childcare responsibilities even when they are in full-time employment.

In nearly two thirds of family units, both partners work, yet according to *Social Trends for 1996/7*, women spend on average three times longer than men on cooking and routine housework, and twice as long on childcare. One UK survey recorded 68 per cent of women and just four per cent of men doing household cleaning, 70 per cent of women and nine per cent of men doing cooking, and 84 per cent of women and three per cent of men doing washing and ironing. The 1994 Mintel survey *Men 2000* concluded that only one in fifty men conform to the 'New Man' image. It found that in nearly three quarters of households the woman was still responsible for cooking, shopping and food preparation.

Mintel identified one in five men qualifying for 'Newish Man', being wholly or mainly responsible for one household task. A further third were 'semi-sharers' offering some help in the household. Only 13 per cent of 'Newish Men' were in paid work. On average, they were found to spend around fifteen hours a week less than women on domestic tasks, and to have one and a half hours' more free time on weekdays and three hours more at weekends. Evidence suggests that where men do contribute there is still division into stereotypical male and female roles, with men doing tasks like DIY and car maintenance, and women doing the washing, cleaning and ironing.

> **New Man is being demolished by the culture of the New Lad, the born again man in search of his fags, football and fornication.**
> Helen Wilkinson *The Independent*

Question
'Is the 'New Man' as mythical a creature as the Abominable Snowman?'

Changing attitudes have encouraged more men to take an active interest in childcare, traditionally seen as women's responsibility.

> ❝ While men are reluctant to say that a woman's place is in the home, it is clear from our research that they still expect her to do the housework. ❞
>
> Angela Hughes, Consumer Research Manager, Mintel

HOW HAVE WOMEN'S ROLES CHANGED WITHIN THE FAMILY?

> ❝ Freedoms, especially for women, bring new challenges, which are being fought more in the public arena. Who would have thought that childcare would be a key election issue 50 years ago? ❞
>
> Carolyn Douglas *Exploring Parenthood*

In the last few decades, women's roles within the family have changed due to a range of influences. In the 1950s, the woman's role was primarily to be a good wife and mother, staying at home and taking care of household chores and children while her husband was the breadwinner on whom she was dependent. In 1911, only ten per cent of wives were in paid employment. Half a century later, this figure had quadrupled. Today, the majority of wives and mothers work outside the home and make up half the labour force. In some countries, they need to work to support their families, while in parts of the world, including Japan and the Middle East, they may still be discouraged from working. Even in the West, they may experience difficulties in obtaining adequate childcare, as well as feelings of guilt and stress at trying to 'have it all'.

WOMEN'S RIGHTS

In previous centuries, women were regarded as the property of their husbands. They could be beaten, raped or deserted without having any right to divorce, receive financial support or have access to their children. A woman's rights today vary around the world. A United Nations research study into sexual equality found that Scandinavian countries have the best record on women's rights, with policies designed to counter discrimination, while countries such as Afghanistan, Bangladesh and Pakistan have the worst.

Marital rape is now illegal in many countries, although domestic violence is still widespread. Research studies show that domestic violence accounts for one in four of all reported crimes. Studies carried out in ten countries found that 17 to 38 per cent of women had been assaulted by a partner. Nearly half of murders of women are by a current or former partner and four out of ten homeless women have left home because they were being abused. Pioneering work by women's groups such as the Women's Refuge movement in the 1970s has exposed the issue and led to a number of initiatives, including police domestic violence units and neighbourhood schemes.

> " The feminist agenda is not about equal rights for women. It is about a socialist, anti-family, political movement. "
>
> Pat Robertson, founder of the US Christian Coalition

HOW HAVE CHILDREN'S ROLES CHANGED?

In pre-industrial societies, the family was seen as a unit of production, with parents and children working together to provide food, clothing and shelter. Children were viewed as miniature adults. In the nineteenth century, legislation restricting child labour and the introduction of compulsory state schooling gave children protection as dependents. In the twentieth century, while children are maturing earlier, the time they are dependent on their parents has been extended due to a shortage of jobs and apprenticeships for school leavers, and cuts in grants and funding for further education.

> 66 The fundamental issue for public policy is the nature of the partnership between the family and the state that will enable the increasing number of elderly people to live their final years with autonomy and dignity. 99
>
> Lynda Clarke, quoted in *The Future of Family Care for Older People* HMSO 1995

WHO WILL CARE FOR THE ELDERLY AND DISABLED?

Traditionally, the elderly have played an important role in the extended family, providing childcare and support to wage-earning children. Societies which value the wisdom and experience of age, such as the Hindu and Chinese cultures, tend also to be those with the strongest sense of family duty and responsibility for the elderly. In the West, where the extended family is now less common, the elderly may still play an important role in family life. A 1994 survey in the UK found that nearly a quarter of pre-school age children were cared for by grandparents.

There is growing concern, however, about future provision of care for the elderly as their numbers continue to grow. At the beginning of the twentieth century, average life expectancy was around fifty years. This has increased to seventy-five years for men and eighty for women. Since 1961, the number of people aged over sixty-five in the UK has almost doubled. As the baby boom generation, born after World War II, reaches retirement age, figures will rise sharply. By 2031, one in four of the UK population will be pensioners. This will result in an estimated increase of £60–100 billion in the cost of providing long-term care.

Grandparents often take on the role of childcarers for working parents.

In the 1960s, it was expected that the state would provide care 'from the cradle to the grave' but cuts in the provision of pensions and state care homes mean that more families are shouldering the burden of care, with some forced to give up their inheritance and sell the family home to pay for care. According to recent surveys, families in the US spend approximately $2 billion a month caring for elderly relatives, and more than twenty-two million US households now care for elderly family members, a threefold increase in the last ten years.

As the population ages, divorce rates rise and birth rates decline, there may be fewer potential carers in the future. Age Concern estimates that ten million 'baby boomers', born in the 1960s, will have no family to care for them.

Even in countries like Italy, where extended Catholic families have traditionally cared for their elderly, the low birth rate and growing divorce rate have left many old people without anyone to care for them. One pensioner, Giovanni Beghini, has started a scheme where the elderly commit legacies and part of their pension to a family in return for becoming 'adopted grandparents'. The question of who should care for the elderly is likely to be one of the main concerns of the new millennium.

> **"** In a materially-based society, it is usually the simplest and crudest issue about later-life families that preoccupies us: how can we support so many economically inactive people? **"**
>
> Jon Bernardes *Family Lives*
> Family Studies 1997

Question
Who do you think should pay for care of the elderly – the state or the family?

> **"** Care of the family cannot be hived off as a family responsibility. **"**
>
> Lynda Clarke, Lecturer in Demography,
> Centre for Population Studies

WHAT IS FAMILY THERAPY?

As changing roles have created new tensions and pressures within families, there has been a growth in the number of outside agencies offering help. In the past, family matters were considered private, and were discussed and resolved among members of the extended family. Today, as the influence of the extended family has declined, it has been replaced with organisations which offer family therapy, counselling and mediation services to deal with problems between partners, between parents and children and between siblings.

WHY IS THE DIVORCE RATE RISING?

In recent years, the number of divorces filed each year has reached record levels. Current figures show that in the UK, which recorded the highest divorce rate in Europe in 1991, four out of ten new marriages will end in divorce. Divorce rates are increasing in many countries around the world. In California, USA, one in two marriages now ends in divorce. The lowest rates tend to be in countries or communities where traditional cultural and religious codes still have influence. Catholicism forbids divorce and a divorcee cannot usually marry in a Catholic church. Catholic countries such as Spain, Italy and Portugal have lower rates, as do ethnic minorities such as Muslim communities living in Europe. People who live in communities with committed religious beliefs may stay together because they fear family disapproval and rejection. Marriages are more likely to hold together in spite of unhappiness.

As well as ethnic grouping and religion, divorce rates are affected by a range of factors including age, class and occupation, family experience and status differences between partners. Rates are higher in urban than in rural areas, and where marriages have taken place after only a short relationship. Analysis of the figures shows that teenage marriages are most at risk of breaking up, with half ending in divorce. The rate for eighteen-year-olds is twice that for twenty-one-year-olds. Factors here may include pregnancy being the main reason for marriage,

Divorce rates remain lower in cultures where religious values still exert influence, such as in many Muslim countries.

family disapproval and rejection, financial and housing problems, and immaturity at the time of marriage, leading to an eventual growing apart. Another high-risk group is that of marriages between people from different ethnic groups, where social disapproval from the families and the wider community can put extra strain on a relationship where there are likely to be major differences in culture and background.

As divorce rates continue to rise, the number of marriages each year is declining. One factor is an increase in unmarried couples co-habiting. But recent research shows that these relationships are even more likely to break up. A 1994 report by the Economic and Social Research Council found that co-habitees are four times more likely to separate than married couples.

> We know from US research that family breakdown can have an effect on psychological, educational and social performance many years later, and it can affect the way people become parents themselves.
>
> Maureen Lynch, Family Mediation Scotland

Find out!

What steps could be taken to find out if couples are compatible before they marry? Carry out a survey to find out what people think are the most important factors in a successful relationship.

WHAT ARE THE MAIN FACTORS IN THE RISE IN DIVORCE RATES?

A number of factors have been blamed for the rapid rise in divorce rates. These include changes in the law, changes in social attitudes towards divorce, the loss of religious belief and values and changes in women's expectations through the influence of the feminist movement which emerged in the 1960s.

In the UK, there have been a number of divorce acts during the nineteenth and twentieth centuries, all moving towards the liberalisation of divorce. In 1923, women were given the right to petition for divorce; in 1950, legal aid became available for divorce cases. In the past, divorce was often costly and messy. One partner had to prove before a court of law that the other was guilty of adultery, cruelty or desertion. If the charge of adultery was contested, the spouse hired a private detective to collect evidence.

In 1969, the Divorce Reform Act changed the grounds of divorce from matrimonial offence to irretrievable breakdown. Separation became sufficient grounds for divorce, after two years if both partners consent, or five if there is not mutual agreement. This change in the law has made divorce less public and has eliminated the need to blame one partner, even if the grounds are cruelty or adultery.

Religious and family pressures make divorce taboo in cultures practising arranged marriages. This is a Hindu wedding in India.

Question
If you were in government, what would you do to try and bring the divorce rate down?

Question
Summer holidays and the Christmas holidays are the busiest times of the year for marriage breakdowns. Why do you think this is?

HOW HAVE ATTITUDES TOWARDS DIVORCE CHANGED?

The effect of changes in the law has been an increased acceptance of divorce in society. Divorce no longer attracts the social stigma it used to thirty years ago. Newspapers and television carry frequent reports of the separation and divorce of figures in the public eye, including rock and media stars and royalty. Alongside a change in social attitudes is a decline in the influence of religion. In the UK, only ten per cent of the population now attends church regularly, and religion is no longer the main focus or guiding influence of most people's lives.

> " The family. . .holds within itself the future of society. It is of prime importance that the value of the family, that community based on the indissoluble marriage of a man and a woman, be rediscovered. "
>
> Pope John Paul II, speaking in St Peter's Square, December 1993

> **"** One of the saddest aspects of the breakdown of family life is the way it reinforces disadvantage and underachievement. The absence of a coherent family policy can mean disaster for those on the lowest incomes, where unstable relationships and insecurity also spell poverty. **"**
>
> David Blunkett, then Shadow Health Secretary, *The Times* 10 November 1993

More than 75 per cent of divorce petitions are brought by women. In the past, marriage was primarily a financial arrangement, with women dependent on their husbands. Two generations ago, the father was still regarded as head of the household and mothers were expected to stay at home and keep house. Many people regarded divorce as morally wrong, and women were not in a position to support themselves if their marriage ended. Many women were forced to remain in 'empty shell' marriages because they could not support themselves. Today, women are educated to higher levels and the majority of wives and mothers work. In 1994, women made up a majority of the workforce, bringing them opportunities for financial independence. Many women no longer see marriage as their only option. They look to their own careers for status, security and fulfilment, and no longer expect marriage to last for the rest of their lives. Changes in the divorce laws, family planning and the influence of feminist ideas have all given them more control over their own lives, dramatically changing attitudes to marriage and divorce.

WHAT ARE THE EFFECTS OF DIVORCE?

Divorce is arguably the most stressful event, next to a death, in a family. Sociologists have identified the stages as 'emotional divorce' when tensions and conflict build between partners, followed by 'legal divorce', then 'economic divorce', as assets and property are divided. If there are children involved, there is also 'co-parental divorce', when issues such as residency and contact orders must be decided. Finally, there is 'community divorce' when the couple's relationships with family, friends and the wider community change. Research shows that in spite of the greater acceptance of divorce in society today, many people still feel a sense of failure and experience emotional disturbance following divorce. The extended family, including grandparents, uncles and aunts, may also feel a sense of loss.

In the UK, seven out of ten divorcing couples have children. More than 150,000 children each year experience the divorce of their parents. Currently, around one in four children go through family break-up before they reach the age of sixteen. If current trends continue, this figure is projected to rise to 28 per cent of children. Parents can decide between themselves on residency and contact, but if they cannot agree there has to be a court hearing. The judge may appoint a court welfare officer, who is a trained social worker, to meet the child and parents. The judge will then issue a court order based on the court welfare officer's report. More than half of divorced fathers have no contact with their children within two years of divorce. This may be due to geographical distance, the distress caused by occasional meetings, or because of tensions caused by relationships with new partners and feelings of divided loyalty.

> **"** The children of divorce are downwardly mobile. They are less likely to marry, more likely to divorce if they do marry, and in the case of females, more likely to become lone parents in their turn. **"**
>
> Patricia Morgan *Farewell to the Family?* 1995

Question

What can parents do to make it easier for their children when they divorce?

> **"** Every increase in the divorce rate results in greater familiarity with divorce as a solution to marital problems, more willingness to use it and to make legislative provision for its aftermath. The pressure on the divorce system leads to a relaxation of practice and procedure in divorce, then a call for a change in the law in order to bring it into line with reality, and then to yet another increase in divorce. **"**
>
> Ruth Deech *Divorce Dissent: Dangers in Divorce Reform* 1994

Children appear to be the main victims of divorce. A study by the Joseph Rowntree Foundation in 1994 found that children suffer more when their parents break up, than if they remain together unhappily. Children whose families had broken up were more likely to suffer low self-esteem, difficulties with friends and at school, and a range of health problems.

Research studies in the UK and the US have found that children of divorce are more likely to underachieve educationally, to experience unemployment and poverty in later life, to suffer poor health, mental illness and even suicide, and to become criminals. One recent medical report claims that bitter divorces can stunt the growth of children. Research showed that children brought up in turbulent homes were twice as likely to be shorter than average by the age of seven. The majority remained shorter all their lives. Scientists believe that childhood stress produces chemicals in the brain which can interfere with the release of growth hormones.

'The divorce inheritance' includes a greater likelihood for children to get divorced themselves in later life. Some experts believe that this is because they have grown up to accept divorce, but others claim that the psychological insecurity and instability produced by family break-up produces divorce-prone individuals.

CAN MEDIATION HELP?

As the number of divorces continues to rise, there has been a growth in the numbers of counselling and mediation agencies which aim to help families through the trauma of family break-up. Organisations like Relate and the Family Mediation Service offer advice and counselling. Pressure groups like Families Need Fathers offer support and lobby MPs on behalf of separated, divorced or unmarried parents. The Family Law Act of 1996 proposes a 'cooling off' period for couples of at least a year, or longer if there are children, before divorce can be finalised. During this time couples would attend information sessions and be encouraged to see mediators to help resolve their problems. The government has also allocated £3 million to fund marriage support and research agencies in their efforts to promote stability in relationships where couples are planning to marry.

> ❝ The main difference between divorce and bereavement is that during a divorce period there is no specified 'time of loss' as there is with a death. ❞
>
> Rosemary Wells *Helping Children Cope With Divorce* 1993

Women get custody of children in 80 per cent of divorce cases. Why do you think this is?

Mediation and counselling are increasingly seen as ways of attempting to resolve marital problems.

WHAT IS A STEPFAMILY?

Stepfamilies are formed after separation, divorce or bereavement. When one adult marries another who already has a child, they legally become that child's step-parent. If both partners have children, the child will have stepbrothers or stepsisters. Stepfamilies are sometimes called 'reconstituted' families or 'reordered' families because they are made up from members of different families living together as a new family unit.

As the number of divorces and remarriages continues to rise, so does the number of stepfamilies. One in three marriages is now a second marriage for one or both partners. In the UK, an estimated 18 million adults and children are in stepfamilies. Figures in 1995 showed that four per cent of stepfamilies include children from both parents' previous relationships. In nearly nine out of ten stepfamilies, the children are from their mother's previous relationship – this is because most children stay with their mother after divorce or separation. Co-habiting couples account for about a third of all stepfamilies with children.

Stepfamilies tend to be larger than most, with an average 2.3 rather than 1.9 dependent children. About 800,000 children in the UK are currently living in stepfamilies.

A growing number of children face the upheaval and readjustment created by divorce and remarriage.

A growing number have relationships with two stepfamilies, because divorce rates for second marriages are higher than average. If current trends continue, one in eight children will live in a stepfamily.

Studies show that one in two stepfamilies will break up. Stepfamilies are relatively unstable, with high divorce rates, due to a range of problems. These can include economic hardship, due to the need to provide maintenance for children from previous relationships.

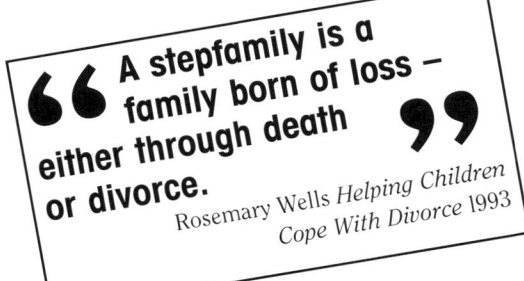

> **A stepfamily is a family born of loss – either through death or divorce.**
>
> Rosemary Wells *Helping Children Cope With Divorce* 1993

> **Stepfamilies are the extended families of the 1990s. We are beginning to see them not as second-best but as a reinvestment in family life. It can be a place where children have four interested adults. Step-parents who make it clear that it's ok to have different ways of doing things between parents will raise more flexible and tolerant children.**
>
> Cheryl Williams, National Stepfamilies Association

Question
'Stepfamilies are the extended families of the 1990s.' Do you think this is true?

WHAT PROBLEMS DO STEPFAMILIES FACE?

Like all families, stepfamilies have their own joys and their own troubles, but because they are reconstituted families, they can bring special problems of adjustment. Children often feel jealousy at having to share their natural parent with a new partner, or with stepbrothers or sisters. If their stepfamily is large, they may feel cramped in the home. They may feel they do not belong to the new family set-up and they may feel confusion and guilt about their relationship with their absent birth parent. They may also feel that their new step-parent is overly strict with them, or behaves unfairly to them, especially when their birth parent is not around.

Children who continue to see their absent birth parent may be regularly moving between two households. These may have different kinds of food, rules and habits. They may have different space and facilities and many children find the transition between two families confusing and disruptive. Family occasions, such as birthdays and Christmas, can be especially difficult. Children may feel torn between their natural parents on special days and holidays.

Step-relationships involve divided loyalties and there can be problems of discipline with a new step-parent. 'You're not my real mother/father,' is a common response. The step-parent may in turn feel jealousy and resentment of his or her partner's relationship with their natural children. There can be special problems if they are not used to being a parent. They may feel threatened or even humiliated by the children. Some reports suggest that same-sex relationships, those between stepmothers and stepdaughters or stepfathers and stepsons, can be the most problematic, especially during the child's adolescence. Marital breakdown and the arrival of a new partner is a common cause of teenagers leaving home. The young person may be harbouring feelings of guilt that it was because of them that their natural parent left home, and they may feel pushed out by their parent's new relationship. A recent survey showed that in half of all cases of young homeless people, a new partner had come into the family.

The arrival of a new baby in a stepfamily can also create problems of jealousy and resentment from existing children. They may feel that they are being rejected and pushed out by the stepfamily. A third of all callers to the Stepfamily Counselling Service have children under five years old, and one in seven callers have a pregnancy or a child under the age of two in the family.

The extended family, including grandparents, may also face problems of adjustment. When a separated or divorced parent forms a new partnership or moves away, grandparents of the absent parent may find themselves excluded. This can be especially painful if their former son- or daughter-in-law becomes hostile towards them, and prevents them having any contact or access to the children.

Question

'Grandparents are the forgotten victims of divorce and remarriage.' Why do you think this is?

Teenagers may find it especially difficult to adjust to the new living arrangements and relationships demanded by stepfamilies.

incomer. Myths and fairytales still have a powerful hold over the imagination, and many stepmothers may feel they have to fight to disprove stereotyped ideas about their role in the family.

> " Neither the myth of the wicked stepmother, nor the getting together of two households to make one big 'Happy Family' describe the harsh reality of being a stepchild for most children. "
>
> Rosemary Wells *Helping Children Cope With Divorce* 1993

> " Research shows that stepfamilies can be very good for children, but it may help to give proper time for adjustment. It appears it can take a year or two years for children to adjust to having just one parent, then a further two to five years to be ready for a new one. "
>
> Erica De'Ath *Stepfamily*

MYTHS AND STEREOTYPES

ABUSE IN THE STEPFAMILY

Western societies' emphasis on physical and personality resemblance to birth parents creates built-in problems for stepfamilies. 'Isn't he like his father?' or 'She is just like you' are age-old ways of reinforcing a sense of inheritance and lineage. For stepfamilies, this can create feelings of confusion and rejection and a sense of not belonging.

Step-parents battle against the stereotypes represented in myths and fairytales. The wicked stepmother is the demon figure in many fairytales such as 'Snow White' and 'Cinderella'. She is seen as the usurper of the natural mother, who may have died tragically, leaving her husband and children at the mercy of the wicked and predatory

In the UK, between 150 and 200 children die of neglect or child abuse every year. Thousands more suffer physical or emotional abuse. According to the NSPCC's annual register, the reported number of child abuse cases rose by 30 per cent a year in the early 1980s. The charity Childline, which opened its helplines in the UK in 1986, recorded about 5,000 calls in the first forty-eight hours. Children are known to be more at risk in families where there is unemployment or low wages and conflict between parents. Some studies have suggested that there may be increased risks of abuse in stepfamilies.

A 1992 survey *Child Abuse Trends in England and Wales* found that there were ten times as many cases as average of child abuse for children living with a father substitute. Stepfathers were more likely to abuse sexually. Live-in boyfriends or partners of the natural mother were more likely to be physically violent towards her children. Another research study, in the US, recorded one in six women as being abused by their stepfather, compared to one in forty women who had been abused by their natural father.

Based on cases reported to social services, the evidence suggests that nearly 20 per cent of physical injury cases, and 25 per cent of sexual abuse cases involve stepfathers or boyfriends of the child's natural mother. In another disturbing study by the Canadian social scientists Daly and Wilson, which used material from Canada, the US, England and Wales, it was found that children under the age of two are seventy times more likely to be killed by step-parents than natural parents.

These statistics remain controversial and difficult to analyse. Some experts point out that cases which come to the attention of the authorities are likely to involve families disadvantaged by problems such as a history of unemployment, domestic violence or mental illness. Many more cases of child abuse may remain unreported. Figures also show that around a third of all cases of sexual abuse involve the natural father; about three per cent involve the natural mother. In calls to Childline about sexual abuse, close to one in four involved a natural father, one in ten a male acquaintance of the family, and one in fourteen a stepfather. Two out of five young homeless people interviewed reported abuse by a parent or step-parent.

Organisations like Childline and the NSPCC and professionals including doctors, health visitors, psychiatrists and social workers continue to carry out research and investigations into child abuse. If social

> **" Living in a stepfamily is the single most important risk factor for severe child maltreatment yet discovered. "**
> Margot Wilson and Martin Daly, McMasters University, Ontario

Child abuse can be a tragic consequence of relationship difficulties within stepfamilies.

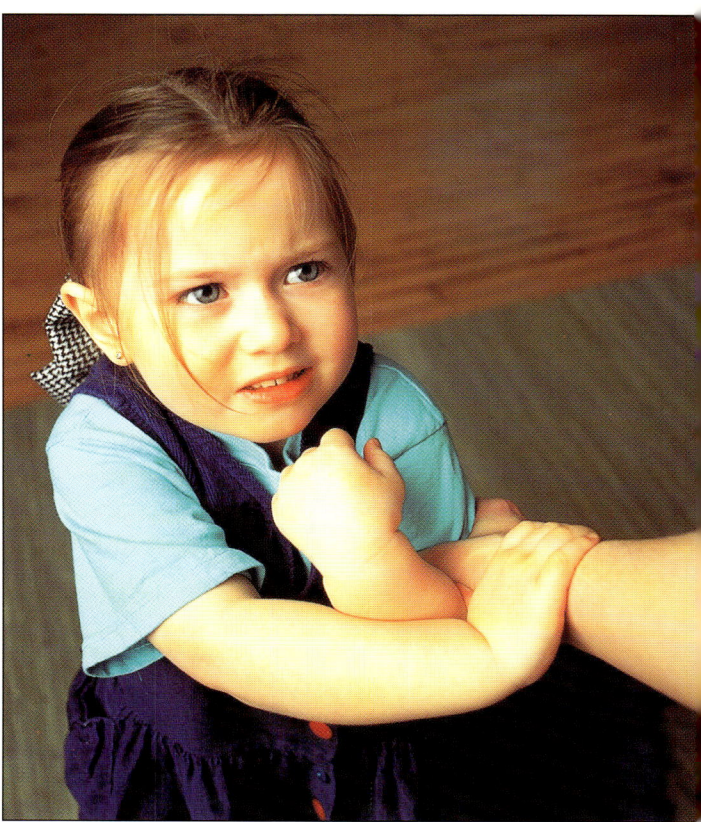

workers believe a child is being abused within the family, they can inform the police, who have powers to investigate and prosecute the abuser. If a child remains at risk, the courts may issue a care order, making the local authority legally responsible for the care of that child.

> 66 Alongside the nuclear family of parents and their children, a new social organisation is developing: the extended network of step-parents, stepchildren, cousins, aunts, uncles and grandparents. It is a grouping that is simply reflecting demographics, expanding and adapting to increased rates of divorce and remarriage. 99
>
> *The Independent* 17 November 1996

DO FAMILIES NEED FATHERS?

In Western societies, there has been a dramatic increase in lone-parent households during the last two decades. The UK has one of the highest proportions of lone-parent households in Europe. Between 1971 and 1997, the number of lone-parent households in the UK trebled to 1.6 million, and the number of children living in lone-parent households rose from one million to 2.3 million. According to 1997 figures, more than one in five of all families with dependent children in the UK are now headed by a lone parent; in the US the figure is one in four. Around a third of all children will experience living in a lone-parent family by the time they are sixteen.

As recently as the 1960s, there was no accepted term for, and no official estimate for, the number of lone-parent families. Social change began in the 1960s with an increase in the number of lone-parent households, and criticism of family policy by social researchers and pressure groups like Gingerbread. Lone-parent households can be formed by:

- parents getting separated or divorced
- a parent dying
- co-habiting parents separating
- an unmarried woman having an unplanned pregnancy from a casual relationship
- a woman choosing to become a lone parent.

Day childcare is increasingly needed by lone parents who go out to work.

A mother heads 90 per cent of lone-parent families. They account for nearly twenty per cent of all households, compared with just two per cent headed by a lone father.

According to 1997 figures, two thirds of lone mothers have been married and are divorced, separated or widowed. Until the 1980s they accounted for the main increase in numbers of lone-parent families. But a report from the Family Policy Studies Centre in July 1992 found that in the late 1980s there was a sharp rise in the number of young single women choosing to have children alone. Between 1961 and 1993, while the birth rate within marriage declined, birth rates outside marriage soared from six per cent to nearly 40 per cent and the percentage is still rising.

More women are choosing to become lone parents, sometimes having several children and supporting themselves quite independently of male partners.

> 66 We have to expect people to see there needs to be a contract between a father and mother to stay together to bring up a child they created. 99
>
> Tom Sackville, then Junior Health Minister, 1993

Question
'Illegitimacy produces an underclass for one compelling practical reason having nothing to do with morality or the sanctity of marriage. Namely, communities need families; communities need fathers.'
(Charles Murray, *The Sunday Times*, 1989.)
Do you agree?

WHY ARE LONE-PARENT HOUSEHOLDS INCREASING?

The rapid rise in the number of lone-parent households reflects a dramatic shift in social attitudes since the 1960s. One of the fastest growing ideas in the last thirty years is the belief that no given lifestyle should be seen as superior or inferior to any other. This has resulted in an increased acceptance of divorce and the loss of stigma against illegitimacy and 'unmarried mothers'. These are some of the main factors which may have contributed to the rise in the number of lone-parent families:

- a decline in the popularity of marriage: 1995 figures in the UK were the lowest for more than fifty years
- a rise in the number of co-habiting partners: in the UK one in ten adults is currently co-habiting and these relationships are known to be less stable than marriage
- a loss of social stigma against illegitimacy and unmarried mothers, with a growing number of public figures providing role models
- an increase in sexual activity among young people and a rise in the number of teenage pregnancies, often through casual or unstable relationships – nearly 90 per cent of teenage mothers are unmarried
- a rapid rise in divorce rates since the 1970s
- changes in women's roles, bringing women more independence and making women feel empowered to leave unsatisfactory marriages or to set up households on their own
- a welfare system which provides access for lone mothers to houses, welfare benefits and tax allowances
- a rise in the number of older, financially secure women choosing to become lone parents.

> 66 As the web of links between crime and the absence of fathers becomes clearer, the community aspect of the problem will loom even larger: it is not just whether any given family is fatherless, but whether the neighbouring families are also fatherless. 99
> Charles Murray *The Sunday Times* November 1993

> 66 Single-parent families are one of the biggest social problems of our day. If someone is old enough to father a child, he should be old enough to help bring it up. 99
> John Redwood, then Welsh Secretary, speech in Cardiff 1993

Question
In spite of better and earlier sex education, teenage pregnancies in the UK are rising. Why do you think this is?

WHO PAYS FOR LONE-PARENT FAMILIES?

Over the last twenty years, UK state expenditure on lone parents has risen an average ten per cent a year. In 1994, the total cost of benefits to lone parents reached £8.5 billion, or nine per cent of the social security budget. By 2000, it is estimated that there will be 1.7 million lone parents in the UK, and eight out of ten of them will be claiming benefits. Lone parents are often restricted to the lowest paid jobs, and surveys show they receive more than half of their income from the state. Only around a third receive maintenance from former partners. They are less likely to receive support when their relationship has been casual. In 1989, while 40 per cent of divorced mothers received maintenance from former husbands, only 14 per cent of single mothers received payments. They are less likely to know who or where the father is, or to want him to support their children.

In 1990, Margaret Thatcher announced the Conservative government's plans for the Child Support Act, which was designed to trace absent fathers and make them legally responsible for maintenance payments for their children. The Child Support Agency (CSA) was given powers to investigate income tax records and enforce payments, deducting them directly from wages where necessary. It aimed to reduce lone parents' long-term dependency on the state, saving £500 million a year in benefits. It has remained controversial legislation, opposed by groups like Families Need Fathers, who believe some fathers have been driven to financial hardship, and even suicide, by the demands of the CSA.

Some people believe that lone parents need more help, such as better childcare and child benefits, but others believe they have become 'wedded to the state', locked into long-term dependency. A controversial BBC *Panorama* programme in 1994 highlighted the issue of single women becoming pregnant to get priority on council housing lists. The Labour government has introduced new childcare schemes and allowances for childcare costs in an attempt to encourage more lone parents back into work.

Find out!
How much does it cost to care for a baby? Find out the cost of essentials like baby food, nappies and baby care products and estimate the average weekly cost.

> **We seem to be on the verge of an unprecedented social experiment, considering that there has been no known human society built upon the mother/child unit.**
>
> Patricia Morgan *Farewell to the Family?* 1995

WHAT ARE THE REAL COSTS OF LONE-PARENT FAMILIES?

Some people see the rise in lone-parent families as a welcome sign of social tolerance and choice in how people live today. Lone parenthood has long been acceptable in societies like Afro-Caribbean communities, and feminists stress the positive aspects for women who have been abused or exploited by men.

But others see the breakdown of the traditional nuclear family as responsible for a range of social problems, including vandalism, drugs and delinquency. In their 1992 work, *Families without Fatherhood*, the sociologists Dennis and Erdos associate fatherless children with anti-social behaviour, educational underachievement and criminality. Charles Murray, who has written about lone-parent families as an 'underclass' locked into welfare dependency, refers to children as young as eighteen months playing unsupervised in the streets in inner city areas. These children have irregular, late bedtimes which affect their performance at school, and truancy, drugs and crime quickly become their lifestyle.

Police figures show that areas with high birth rates outside marriage also have high levels of poverty and crime. In the US, three quarters of juveniles in State Reform institutions are from fatherless families. Research studies in the US suggest that children brought up by a lone mother are four times more likely to drop out from school, become delinquent or commit suicide than those brought up by a lone father. Some people argue that children need the role model and discipline provided by a father. But others argue that social problems are the result of poverty and hardship rather than lone parenthood.

> 66 There is little evidence to support the assertion that lone parenthood – or lone motherhood – is itself a direct cause of underachievement of children, juvenile delinquency, crime or general social disintegration. 99
>
> *The Family Way*, report by the Institute for Public Policy Research 1990

The cost of bringing up a child can mean that many lone parents experience poverty and hardship.

How can changes in the law help?

Under existing law, unmarried fathers have no rights or responsibilities for their child unless both parents have signed an agreement in court, or the father has obtained a parental responsibility order from court. The father has no say in a child's upbringing, surname or adoption by another parent.

Some experts argue that non-resident fathers should have greater legal rights and responsibilities towards their children. They believe that children would benefit financially and psychologically if natural fathers shared child benefits and residence orders with the mothers. The government has proposed making birth parents jointly responsible for their children, regardless of marital status. A report from the Institute of Public Policy Research published in 1998 suggested new initiatives, such as 'child commitment ceremonies', making both parents aware of their rights and responsibilities when a birth is registered.

Question
Some people think there should be cuts in benefits to discourage people from becoming lone parents. What do you think?

Question
'The only real family is the mother and her baby. Everyone else is peripheral.' (Clare Rayner, *The Jewish Chronicle*, 1994.)
What do you think?

WHAT IS THE FUTURE FOR THE FAMILY?

Statistics show that the family is continuing to change and evolve as we enter the twenty-first century. Marriage and birth rates are declining, while the numbers of people divorcing or choosing to co-habit continue to increase. Current trends suggest that it will be common for people to experience periods of change and instability in their relationships. More people may practise 'serial monogamy', having a succession of marriages or partners. As social attitudes change, science is also challenging traditional concepts of parenthood and the family. New reproductive techniques mean that people who could not previously have children, including post-menopausal women and homosexuals, may be given the chance to become parents. 'Granny mothers' and cases of 'DIY lesbian pregnancies' and homosexuals fostering or adopting children have become controversial news.

> ❝ Heterosexuality, marriage and having children are. . .all part of the Western patriarchal parcel of rules for appropriate sexual relations and behaviour between men and women. Indulging in one without accepting the rest of the 'parcel' has been, and still is, widely condemned. ❞
>
> D. Gittins *The Family in Question: Changing Households and Familiar Ideologies* 1992

Question
Do you think children need a male and a female parent to provide role models? If so, why?

Some childless couples are able to adopt an orphaned child from overseas, such as this British couple with a little girl from Romania.

DO SAME-SEX COUPLES HAVE THE RIGHT TO BE PARENTS?

The late twentieth century has brought increasing awareness of gay rights, including the right of homosexuals to parent children. In Europe and the US, there has been a growing number of reports of lesbian pregnancies and gay couples applying to foster or adopt children. Some people see this as a choice that should be available, and a way of counteracting patriarchal institutions like the conventional nuclear family. Others criticise it as an attack on traditional family values and voice concerns for the welfare of children raised by same-sex couples. Some people believe there should be legislation to prevent homosexuals adopting children. They think that children of same-sex couples may be bullied at school, and may be more likely to grow up as homosexuals. Others think that homosexuals should have the same rights to adopt as heterosexual couples. Childcare agencies point out that there is a shortage of foster parents, especially for children with behavioural or learning difficulties. They are backed by US research studies which have found no evidence that children of same-sex couples are disadvantaged in any way, or are more likely to become homosexuals.

Newspapers have reported a 'worldwide lesbian baby boom', the majority born through artificial insemination, using sperm from a sperm bank or donor known to the mother. Fertility clinics are free to dictate their own policy on same-sex parenting, although they must take into account the couple's social and economic background and the 'potential child's need for a father'. The Bridge Fertility Centre in London estimates that currently around one in ten of its clients are lesbians. As well as the moral and ethical arguments surrounding homosexual parenting, legal issues have been raised. In the UK, under current law, a non-biological parent has no legal rights in the upbringing of a child.

Find out!

What do you see as the future for the family in the twenty-first century? What changes do you think will take place during your lifetime?

The adoption of children by single-sex couples challenges centuries-old views of the family.

> **We should cease regarding lesbian households as all the same. Like heterosexual households, they differ greatly. Perhaps it is the quality of family relationships and the pattern of upbringing that matters for psychosexual development, and not the sexual orientation of the mother.**
>
> Susan Golombok,
> Reader at the City University

GRANNY MOTHERS

Mothers are getting older. As life expectancies rise, more women are choosing to postpone childbearing. Between 1981 and 1991, there was a 50 per cent increase in the number of women in their late thirties giving birth. The number of mothers over the age of forty has also risen by 60 per cent in a decade. Advances in reproductive technologies including *in vitro* fertilisation and embryo transplants mean that it is now possible for women to give birth after the menopause. *In vitro* fertilisation is a technique for fertilising an ovum or egg outside the womb. Doctors are divided on the ethics of giving IVF to post-menopausal

women. In 1993, when a fifty-nine-year-old woman gave birth to test-tube twins at Professor Severino Antinori's fertility clinic in Italy, it raised a storm of controversy. Dr John Marks, formerly of the British Medical Association (BMA), spoke of his horror at a case that 'bordered on the Frankenstein syndrome'. Dr Stuart Horner, of the BMA's ethical committee, opposed the birth on the grounds that the twins would grow up with parents of 'a wholly foreign generation'. The Roman Catholic Church condemned Dr Antinori for his 'horrifying work in pre-fabricating orphans'.

In the UK, IVF clinics are licensed by the Human Fertilisation and Embryology Authority (HFEA). Although there is no legal upper age limit for fertility treatment, doctors are required to take it into account for the welfare of both the mother and the potential child. In the early 1990s, the number of over-forty-fives receiving IVF rose from 143 to 360, although some clinics refuse treatment to women over forty. This has led to cases of women lying about their age to obtain treatment. Some experts argue that women should have the same rights to older parenthood as men. They are supported by research studies which show that older mothers communicate better with young children. Others are concerned for the welfare of children born to women old enough to be grandmothers.

Question
'Every woman has the right to have a child. Who says it's not right for a woman to have a child at 55? A man can have a child at that age and everyone says "Isn't he clever?"...It's a disgrace.'
(Professor Severino Antinori, *The Independent on Sunday*, 1993.)
What do you think?

An estimated 50,000 embryos are stored in liquid nitrogen in fertility clinics in the UK. In 1996 nearly 4,500 were destroyed after reaching the five-year maximum storage limit set by the HFEA in 1991. This was opposed by anti-abortion and pro-life groups. Embryos created since 1996 may now be stored for up to ten years with written consent from the parents. At present, they cannot be used without the consent of both parents, but there have been cases of separated parents fighting for legal control of their embryos.

THE ISSUES SURROUNDING IN VITRO FERTILISATION

Since the first test-tube baby was born in the UK in 1978, there have been thousands of babies born through IVF and other assisted fertility treatments. An estimated 30,000 women worldwide are currently receiving fertility treatment, at a cost of £230 million a year. The increasing use of IVF has raised a number of controversial issues:

- should single women be given IVF?
- do all couples, married or unmarried, heterosexual or gay, have the right to be parents?
- should IVF be given to older women?
- with the global population rising, should multiple births through IVF be permitted?

Recent cases have highlighted some of the issues surrounding IVF. These include the controversial case of a black woman who chose to be impregnated with eggs from a black donor because she had decided she did not want to have a mixed-race child by her white partner.

66 The essence of IVF, for mothers of whatever age, is that it has granted them a personal freedom. Medical science has done its duty. It has offered women choice as it long ago offered them the choice of painless childbirth. 99
Simon Jenkins *The Times* 29 December 1993

66 IVF 15 or 16 years ago was considered to be abhorrent. It is now commonplace. Ethics and opinions change with time. 99
Dr Peter Brinsden, Director of the Bourn Hall Clinic

Question
Do you think that IVF should be given to women after their menopause?

> **If scientists can now help infertile or older women to have normal babies, good for science. Such women are no more 'defying nature' than is abortion or IVF or hormone replacement therapy.**
>
> Simon Jenkins *The Times* 29 December 1993

DESIGNER BABIES

Scientists are now making advances in human embryology which are raising new moral and ethical issues. The shortage of donor eggs for infertile couples has led to research into using eggs from female foetuses or dead women. In 1994 the HFEA published a document on work in transplanting eggs from aborted foetuses into the wombs of host mothers. This could result in a generation of 'skipped mothers': a child's biological mother may never have existed.

Many pro-life campaigners have opposed the research, but others argue that the current shortage of donor eggs means that some women have to wait up to five years for fertility treatment.

In 1993 the US scientist Dr Jerry Hall carried out cloning of human embryos. The embryo is divided into four at the four-cell stage, allowing all four parts to develop into viable embryos sharing the same genes. Dr Hall split single embryos into twins and quadruplets. Some people argue that this technique could provide badly needed embryos for infertile couples. Others fear that this sort of research will undermine our concept of the uniqueness of each human being. They also believe that it could lead to 'human eugenics', where genes are manipulated to create people with perfect looks and intelligence. Advances in medical science and reproductive technologies could radically change our concepts of the family, and the individuals within it, in the future.

> **We cannot stop the advance of science, but we can decide how we want to limit its effects.**
>
> Sir Colin Campbell, Chairman of the HFEA, January 1994

Families Need Fathers
134 Curtain Road
London EC2A 3AR
0171 613 5060

The Family Policy Studies Centre
231 Baker Street
London NW1 6XE
0171 486 8211

Gingerbread
Association for One Parent Families
16 Clerkenwell Close
London EC1
0171 336 8183

Help the Aged
St James' Walk
Clerkenwell Green
London EC1R 0BE
0171 253 0253

National Council for One Parent Families
255 Kentish Town Road
London NW5 2LX
0171 267 1361

National Family Mediation
9 Tavistock Place
London WC1H 9SN
0171 383 5993

National Stepfamily Association
Chapel House
18 Hatton Place
London EC1N 8RU
0171 209 2460

Parents at Work
Murray House
45 Beech Street
London EC2Y 8AD
0171 628 3565

Relate International
Herbert Gray College
Little Church Street
Rugby CV21 3AP
01788 573 241

AUSTRALIA

Commonwealth Department of Health and Family Services
GPO Box 9848
Melbourne Vic 3000
Tel: (03) 9285 8888

Commonwealth Department of Health and Family Services
1 Oxford Street
Darlinghurst NSW 2010
Tel: (02) 9263 3662

Commonwealth Department of Health and Family Services
340 Adelaide Street
Adelaide SA 5000
Tel: (07) 3360 2555

Commonwealth Department of Health and Family Services
152 St Georges Terrace
Perth WA 6000
Tel: (08) 9346 5111

Australian Institute of Family Studies
300 Queen Street
Melbourne Vic 3000
Tel: (03) 9608 6888

Family Mediation Centre
367 Princes Highway
Noble Park Vic 3174
Tel: (03) 9547 6466

Good Shepherd Youth and Family Services
117 Johnston Street
Collingwood Vic 3066
Tel: (03) 9419 5477

FURTHER READING

Isabel Allen (ed). **The Future of Family Care for Older People.** HMSO, 1995.

Erica de'Ath. **Teenagers Growing Up in a Stepfamily.** Stepfamily Publications, 1990.

Jon Bernardes. **Family Studies.** Routledge, 1997.

Joanna Bogle. **Families for Tomorrow.** Fowler Wright, 1991.

Jonathan Bradshaw. **Lone Parent Families in the UK.** HMSO, 1991.

Suzie Hayman. **Relate Guide to Second Families.** Ebury Press, 1996.

Nik Jorgensen. **Investigating Families and Households.** Collins Educational, 1995

Tim Kahn. **Learning to Step Together: building and strengthening stepfamilies.** Stepfamily Publications, 1995.

Claire Salisbury and Cheryl Walters. **All Together Now: what to expect when stepfamilies get together.** Stepfamily Publications, 1995.

INDEX

Index